Tish Oakwood

Earth to Eagle

Published by Dolman Scott Ltd 2020

Cover illustration by Rachel Beard

ISBN 978-1-911412-87-8

Dolman Scott Ltd
www.dolmanscott.co.uk

Dedication

For Jean - she read them all

Contents

my little rusty

my little rusty patched and leaking shed
that keeps its oil and bits of engine smells
as if it can't abide the change that is inherent
in all things is full of crispy sunshine
open tree blue skies and wagtail hops
this february day as i drape the rug
over a chair to dry in front of
the spluttering heater and arrange myself
upon the least fusty cushion
to write

when you are married you pickle

she's an alto and she's never attempted marmalade
it would stick in her hair and is such a lot of bother
like the onions i tried to pickle once because i was
married and had young children and isn't that
what i was meant to do? spend hours
peeling
boiling
pickling
and
simultaneously
changing
wiping
washing
burping
and getting peed in the eye as though the wife must
atone for whatever unknown sins she or her whole
family may have committed by submerging herself
in the smelliest
teariest
most ugly
and arduous
of mothering
housewifing
tasks
imaginable
and after the peeling and the rounds of cooking and
the changing and the ages of boiling the whole
house reeked for weeks, years even, and the rats
ran off in disgust and eventually so did i
so as she is beyond being a mother of young
children or a spouse to anyone who would hold
her hostage to her duties there is no need for messy
chores unless she chooses such, no need for making
marmalade although it would be more rewarding
but even

more so
would be
to sing alto
in the amen
chorus of
handel's messiah
and then go home and eat lemon curd

it's snowing again

it's snowing again,
some people talk like hailstones
battering my silences

while some are stony silent,
cold not noticing
my drift and slide away

from their frozen heartedness.
it's snowing again
and you my dear,

you are that peace
of settled snow on a still earth -
you shoot no icy word pellets.

it's snowing again,
we could show children
how to craft paper doilies.

do you know any good snow poems?
or polar bear yoga poses?
or snowdrift pudding recipes?

the children are tobogganning
and falling into one another
- let's go out and eat snow!

it's snowing again,
all we need is a magnifying glass
and a snowflake.

it’s snowing again,
time to huddle in with steaming cocoa
and not talk much.

it’s snowing again –
your long arms wrap right around me,
we might melt.

the january one

she drank sparkling wine each month
to forget about the egg on its journey
and how it tinted her view of
cycles and meat, blood and sex
since the day the january one escaped
its holding

it should be the size of a curled up
hiccupping sausage by now
instead of a maggot
swilling noxious in newark
and sherwood district council's
sewage

had it been twins
they might be ready
to chat to each other
like jersey royals
simmering in the pot

jason's mates would be
toasting his virility,
and hers YouTubing
how to knit a tiny weeny
woolly hat

she imagined the wine's bubbles
opening their mouths
in rebuke

one bubble, two, three - one egg
- *and you dropped it*

what style of greetings card would you
choose for a baby that got lost in the post?

as bees do

bee fattened in spotted foxglove. beyond her
muffled reverie screeching tyres, crunching metal, screams
on screams and a momentary stilled silence.

bee hovered, observed the mother lifting her babies out,
setting them sobbing on the evian plastic
rotting burger-scrapped july-burnt verge.

bee crapped, ridding herself of excess heat, more
interested in the globular queen and a cloud of mating-
minded drones competitively surging till the after-
smell of sex and suicide was in the air.
a cup of steam was handed to the dying human drones.

bee got as far away as she could, noting that
sex in the human as well as the bee world was brutal
resulting in injury and death.

sated and defecated, (buddleia bloomed
and blushed), she watched from beneath her purple perch and
when the glinting shining shards of sunlight strewn
across the road stopped quivering and the tarmac
relaxed into globs of crimson and blurry bluey blackness
and all that was left was snivelling children and
parent drones whose eyes closed and opened,
closed and opened, and the crooked humans were
tumbled into the mad clanging blue eyes flashing
people guzzler that shrieked in the moaning noon
bee let out her sting on the ankle of the paramedic's
foot that crushed her and rolled into a large blot
of smelly rainbows.

snail 1

i'd have liked to have been a girl, perhaps a snail *
but who says i have been neither of those?
a tomboy i was, but a tomboy is by definition
a girl, yes? and surely in the wandering days
although my mother called me packhorse
what with sleeping bag guitar and rucksack
slung around my back and over my shoulder
i could just as well have been a snail, yes?

snail 2

spring snails compete with slugs
slug bugs so small
you would think
they could do no damage

hah!

baby slug bugs
in the baby seedling beds

and guess
who
wins

snail 3

some days the snail is me.

i move around at a snails pace pacing as i go, counting steps,
measuring my achieved distance. i doubt a snail could be
bothered
to do this even if someone suggested it would be good for him.

the snail is me.

snail 4

maybe i should teach the snail population
some maths and logic? i could advertise
my services in lettuce beds and in the gap
between the wall and the window box;
"calling all gastropods! have you considered
how much further you could travel if you just
knew where you were going and how many
days it will take you to get there?"

is ignorance bliss? unhurriedly i ponder

perhaps the primitive two-celled brain
that keeps you fed is sufficient

and who am i to tamper with your evolution?

you win.

snail 5

winning snails. snail races. some people in some places -
particularly norfolk i
understand - race snails. the owners train their competitors and build them up with protein manipulated pea shoots and coach them, give them affirmations to repeat at bedtime, breakfast time, and when they come to a fork in the cabbage patch; *i am the fastest snail in the world, i have everything i need to be a champion, i am a winner, my stamina and speed are legendary, the stainless steel and ribboned tankard stuffed with succulent lettuce leaves shall be mine, shall be MINE!*

who needs wimbledon when you have a racing snail bent on defending his title?

snail 6

i'd have liked to have been a girl, perhaps a snail.
perhaps a girl snail
in a snail skirt

only this girl snail
wouldn't wear skirts
would she

* *prompt from a poem by Sharon Black*

i want a woman who

i want a woman who paints
her room lilac and pink
and bedouin indigo blue
with stars and moons
like the ones her kids
were just too old for
by the time the 1980's
toy shops got to stock them

this woman wears purple
and patches, three scarves
at a time (all different colours –
you'd think they'd clash
but they enliven) and walks
in the dark in case she can hear
the birds chirping
in jupiter's chorus

when she stands and beams
in cloud-light and an owl ruffles
up the needles of the conifer
beside her suddenly she stops
despising the forestry commission

and revels in the right here right
now that only she in the entire
universe has been in – like her insides
feeling the fullness and the rough
of her baby crowning

once my snail

once my snail had four wheels or five if you include the spare
and she took me
from wessex to northumberland without touching a motorway
which is fortunate – she might have got crushed

and living in her though objecting to the taste of diesel i
became the snail

journeying the lanes with grass
growing up the middle suited us both as we strayed
westwards for watering at rivers, lake, and even once
close to the sea –
she thought for a moment she was a marine mollusc

at night i raised her striped roof and we dozed, my eye
on the stars, her cephalic tentacle sensing a field of young
barley or a strawberry patch

yes at some point i became the snail

which might on reflection be where
these poems have come from

frozen
i.m. Tom 1980 – 2012, died in police custody

there you are
in my local tesco –
not buying bread
or tulips
not rifling through the onion skins
no
there you are
staring out at me
between
good housekeeping
and the *tv times*
with that face of awful pain
that face
that froze
forever grieved
bewildered

i buy
the *western morning news*
and
extravagantly
the guardian
i read
that your family has been diminished
in the four and a half years
since he died

dim   inished
ish ed   ish ed   ish ed

as the state took ownership
of his body
as the first trial failed
as you watched the footage

over and over
in the courtroom
of your son heavily restrained
by police -
struggling
resisting
suffering
cardiac

arrest

and the verdict
now
un
fathomable
un
thinkable
un
swallowable

as the onions
raw and whole
would have
been
even
had i found you
in tesco with
a shopping list
and a wonky trolley
instead
of underneath
the headline

police cleared
over death of mentally ill prisoner

reeling
dazed
into a frozen future

in a supermarket set poem
i would rather be writing about
frozen fishcakes

easier to thaw
and requiring nothing
more
than a little egg
to put them
back
together
again

solstice

at the dark heart of the year
the marsh is silent. snow
quiets the breath of the earth,
and there is no thaw.

yet, imagine you could wriggle,
claw into the burrows, badgers
setts, and slither deep
on ancient tree roots, further,

boring down in channels now
of molten matter running true
through lithospheric tumblings
as you drop into the innards.

hah! you are the core! (did you
even for one moment believe
that you were separate?). dense
and sightless,

lightless, blacker than
the jackdaw hopping, trapped
in lead and ore since planet first
was born, but wait. awake. what

goads your skin? a heat? in fact
a heat so great it equals that
of suns! and from such source,
did not, *do* not, all energy

and forms originate? including
you? including me? follow
a seeming quiet thing far enough,
sit with it in its pause space, let

it find its way to turn, reverse,
move on, and in the resting
time observe a vibrancy
the heavens knew would

come again, while earth,
reposing, dreams towards
more coloured garb and fields
for harvest, before reflective

snowtime must recur. do not
the sun and swallow,
larkspur, lime, and lovers
all spin to one eternal law?

devon red

think
of triassic rock hulking itself
two hundred and fifty million years
and parting continents
to get here

now
comprehend
the credibility
of love

moon cradle

as there are two moons
cradled child to mother
as the dwarfstar in the gloom
sees each star as brother
as an ordinary tune
is symphony to a lover

so you cradle me
my moon man
so you cradle me

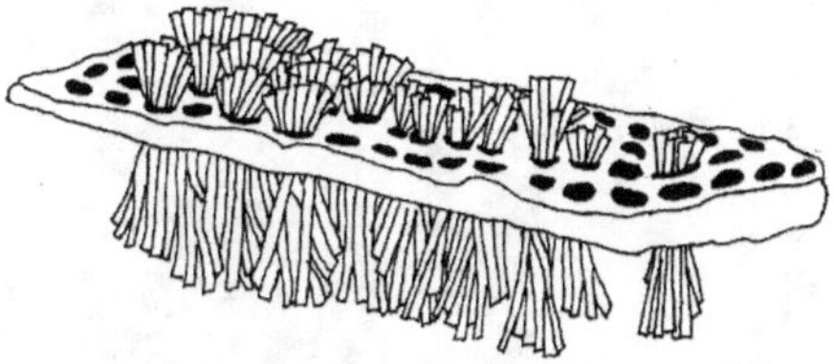

Note: Poem inspired by a Roman Scrubbing Brush

on bristly tiptoes

on bristly tiptoes i walk
all seven hundred and fourteen of me

my caterpillar legs
dancing like tiller girls

hawaiian grass skirted sisters
corralled into line

an army of scarecrows
marching nowhere

pilloried and shorn
for whose entertainment?

who will soil my skirts
or scalp my head

pelt
my steadily asphyxiating neck

with offal, eggs
and ridicule?

for seasons did i grow in fields
until the firmest stoutest stems of me

were dried
and selected to be strangled

and to perform to tuba
and to tympanum

like collared monkeys
on a jewelled chain

you thought i was a toy
for your enthrallment

transient, of straw,
destructible

yet i am here
preserved

with all my scratchety dancing bitches
clean, revered

still an object of fascination
but now held in high esteem

because
i have
survived

nectar and goddesses

she drank honey

because she was a goddess she got away with it

goddesses have privileges like
being able to fly
staying calm in earthquakes
and never having to bleed, defecate,
or argue about putting out the rubbish

in return
they can't experience earthly love or sex
go on holiday to magaluf
gorge on ice cream and cider
or get a master's degree

but drinking honey didn't make her sick

e
ar
th to
eagle
eagles fly
below the
skyline, they bat their wings and beat across the gape of canyon's mouth. what is older than a mountain?
not i, not you, but maybe eagles…….earth to eagle, mountain to dust, dust to wingspan, flap to skyline, sky and moon
to shine through feathers strong, and almost silent. silence in a rockscape, ancient man and woman hunting, squat inside the
cave the woman painted, or the man, red orange ochre palaeolithic pictures, people, creatures, weapons, stick lines
held in by time, burnt in by fire, and, here we come, we techno humans, no
tools, no weap
ons bar our throw
away mobile phones which
do it all
but
oh!
we'll
never
have
an app
for flying
for silence
for the grace of the eagle
will we?

who painted the pictures?

and who made the paint?
what was it made of
and did they walk with it

from place to place?
did they live in the caves
or just pass through?

are the worn smooth rocks
their long ago pillows
like saint john's

not the john who had
the revelation, no,
the one of the cretan cave

who lived on figs and carob
and who some thought of as
an animal so naked

and bent over was he -
and did they have visions
brought on by ritual

and traversing the peaks
barefoot, skin-clad
in fight flight freeze mode

for their eighteen
or twenty five years of life
until low body fat

or the sabre toothed tigers
got them? where were they going?
where were they from?

who did they pray to?
and most of all, most
puzzling of all

why
did they not
depict
eagles?

la mallata

i sit at la mallata
observing
three thousand feet below me
eighteen thousand years
behind me
and thickly forested
inaccessible
canyon walls
dotted with caves
to left and right

above and beyond
just sky
and sky
silent

silent
that is
except for the batting
of eagle's wings
and the clouded
whispers
emanating
from ancient
mountain
deities
appearing there
in secret
and faded images
drawn
in caves
of darkness
and the smile
of the mother goddess
sculpted from mammoth ivory

because creativity and ritual
have sought voice
for as long
and
as wide
as the mountain

primordial
mortals
traversing
impossible
rockscapes
with eagles gliding
soaring
skirring their skies

eagles courting at the turn
of luna
picking up
then dropping and
re
trieving
stones
mid flight
in a two hundred
mile an hour
swoop
to offer
a mate

dive
fly
dance
the empyrean
in unison

spirit eagle
circles
dimensionless vistas

disappear   s

carries invocations
on a wingtip
to the great
sky gods
and
re
turns
with messages to deliver
to the rock locked spear stick
palaeolithic people
in their dreamtime
and because i
fancy
that i too
can hear those intimations
from wind spirit and eagles
eclipses
and speaking mountains
planted into visions
painted onto
rockfaces
translated
into sounds
chanted
drummed
whistled through a bone flute
and whirled in exaltation
twenty millennia later
it could be
that if i

sit
long enough
the canyon
might
move
through
me

i came to the mountain

i came to the mountain with a yen for hunting
treasure esteemed as the stronghold, the rock
and the sparkle, the hue and the splendour our
love has delivered to me, this beginning year. i
found views, i found peace, a butterfly in foxtrot,
and over the rushes a breeze gentle as a baby's
breath in sleeping, and if, as i once read, the
space within is greater than the entire external
universe, then all these things are in us, yes,
and that i could bring none of them home from
the mountain to you gift-wrapped matters not.

the views as wide as the distance an angel
flies speak to the open vistas of our similitude,
to the rising east and the balmy west, the
sizzling south – the true north. not to be
contained in an envelope or on a piece of paper,
stowed in bubblewrap or held in cupped hands;
familiar, and outermost, green, secluded, arid,
grassy, oakish, landslipped, scuppered, fading
blue-ly to the beacons, to the cambrians, so
that the coyly murmuring brook might just be
passed unseen because the mountain is so
look at me grand. dancing marsh fritillary
of calligraphic markings brings a light and
mindful comfort, soft and multi-tufted as moss,
our leafing, the glimpse of a filling gibbous
moon, your kiss to the back of my neck
in passing, eva cassidy in a dewsome dusk.

the peace – ah – lying with you my dearling,
untroubled, unhurried, a peace that parallels
the lull and hush of every mountain ever trod
upon – the grandest, remotest, dinasouric, the
holy, eroded, the rounded, deserted, extinct,

ex-volcanic, the gladed, the windswept, the
lunar, unscalable. and the straw-like rushes
in the breeze speak to me of steadfast depend-
ability, for surely they withstood the winter
winds, the snows, and morning followed
night and sun did rise and spring did come,
and still they sway and swoop and hold their
height on slender stem for yet another season.

our love is these things, yes, and as i write
a bird so small a sprig of heather could quite
fair conceal it dives into the reeds, withdraws,
and hovers on a wingspan then re-settles in
to feed. children's limbs and voices strident,
awed, exuberant, pour out over the ridge, and
at once a small aircraft whose rumble and
hum i have been aware of becomes visible
in great detail above the wiry welsh oak.

this whole panoply speaks to me of our one
year still new pairing birthing. our observing,
emerging, allowing the path to lay its inceptive
stones along the course and the contours, the
dips and the edges of a way we're wending
together, feather light, going somewhere
lemon leaved and melon canopied sometimes
swathed in rose petals, gardened balm and
delight, sometimes cold to footfall, toenails
bending out of line for a moment, but only
a moment. faltering not – the walk of life, one
step, two steps, one wall to scale, one mile
attained by daybreak or by night end, for which
is which and is the demarcation of importance
– and arms for turning to, and bodies frail until
they strengthen, like bellies empty till they're
fed, two hands to meet like beech roots twisting
into one across the decades and yet to always

stay as two, two hearts to strike one drumbeat
rhythm for your voice and mine a forest floor,
our pleaching, this fledged and maiden year.

lost

i came to the canyon
to write another eagle poem
but it was you
who were the eagle

you disappeared
into thin air
although the shaman said
your animals
are hummingbird
and tiger

hummingbird too fragile
and nectar needy

a tiger could
possibly
leap sure footed
on ridges above these
eight hundred metre
almost vertical
rock faces
finding footholds
lithe
keen eyed
like the eagle that
in truth
you weren't

for if you were you would
have seen
me
as i searched for you
and let me see you too

but as you are
and i am
two legged
not striped black and orange
neither
sporting golden
six and a half foot wingspans
flecked with white

we   lost   each   other

i on a rock
not writing but watching
and you in a cave
not flying
or soaring

not screaming
tumbling
toppling

or calling

for me

eagles
agile
swift
oblivious
to the two humans
on the far edges
of their airscape

as it happens
just fifty feet
above and below each other

lost

earth and stone

the earth births me

mud and stone
moss and rockabye foxglove
receive my body in a mother's embrace

laying my head upon a breast
of oak twistings
ash saplings
and spiders climbing rye grass

i wriggle
and find i am alive

weekend

on sunset washed sands
under spindly legs
gulls
secure
their shadows

in pine-sharp woods
to the leeward side of the sun
a puddle undisturbed
becomes
a teeming
ecosphere

peaceful and sated
in your arms
connected at our core
in reverent stillness
- misted field
quietly pulses
in pale sheet lightning
low on the horizon
otherwise
darkness
cocooned

outside of this
this weekend
there need be nothing

divorce

a butchered marriage
sliced into two neat portions
left on a slab
to bleed dry
while the night outside
weeps at the cutting

a cow's heart
takes up her whole mid sector

pierce her through her heart
and you split her into two
almost equal
lumps
of
dead
flesh

milk seeps

other time fog

the light
of the overly lit room
baling out through an open window
comes to rest
fixed in fog
like a surreally hanging stone

your shrinking world

have you noticed how the world shrinks as you get older? not only because you
don't have the physical stamina to stand in airport queues or the strength to
lift suitcases on and off the scales at check-in and then the reclaim belt
but also because place after place is tainted with feelings
you'd rather not re-visit until the needle point of
your life stitches you into the not turkish but
tesco's coffee spilled fabric of your
electric recliner with its caddy
for your mobile and remote
surrounded by photo
albums travel
books and
a clutch
of pad
lock
ed

diar

ie

s

?

ribbons trees equations

girly i never was – tomboy
they labelled me. i didn't mind. i
climbed the ornamental cherry tree

and dreamed it was a beech, a
sequoia, a ladder to another world -
the rooftops, sierra nevada,

the lofty places where i could be
exactly whatever it was i
wanted to be, free

of sticky-out-skirts, ribbons,
and all other encumbrances
imposed upon me.

girls of fluff relished embellishments
and bows. bows ironed, even,
equidistantly symmetrically spotted

yellow, red, or god forbid pink. mother
used to tie my hair with ribbons (they
ended up in knots) and all the fancy satin

in north london never succeeded in
making me a girly girl – i
was going to be a mathematician

> now, i see loud huddles of
> would-be fashionistas
> in the shopping mall
> on their way to escaping
> pubescent androgyny,
> the newly teened
> discussing how to bribe
> a parent

i'll tidy my room. no
that won't work, they'll
never believe me. okay, how
about this.... *i'll*
wash the dishes
for a week, tell you about
my day, give up love island
(as if!) for sculpted
designer nails
and

i'm gonna get breast implants, defo.
we all will, won't we....

see who they can be, these mini-adults
sporting skirts that barely cover not yet
spherical buttocks - sex goddesses, tarts

with belly buttons taut and glinting, and
whore shoes higher than the crown of
the oak i believed i could hover in

and then there are the men
who choose to wear
make-up and a cocktail gown,
bandage their lower
circumferences and apexes,
don size ten stilettos, and
in scented drawers
secret away silicone hips
and frilly, orbicular
infilled bras

– i try to understand this

by climbing trees, teetering on heels,
binding our genitals or pumpkinning

our boobs, we add, subtract, multiply

and slip into some imagined and more
splendid woman-person-girl-she deity-
idealized and idolized-transvestite-hoyden.

are men in petticoats, or five foot
girls in six inch heels not incongruent
then, with the child who resisted ribbons,
asked for trousers (denied), and sat
on a cloud high limb, with a stone, a dream,
and a ball of string in her gymslip pocket?

i, poem

i, poem, i seek you.
the man who penned me,
this is his unburdening tool.
like whittling the willow,
he carefully scrapes off
thin peelings and finds
the nub of you.
then he moves there,
massages your heart
as though he were warming
bread dough.

i, poem, am the utterance
of the man. i say to you
i will strip you naked
to discover my truth,
as brazenly as though
i were an x-ray
to your hiddenness.

i, poem, am the gasp
of the man. on my indrawn breath
i reclaim passion. wanting you,
wanting, with you - his serpent energy,
his rise up and dance - to be fiercely,
concentratedly, directed.

i, poem, i speak for intensity
concealed beneath volcanic field until
breaking free, it steams, sizzles,
and settles. you, open mind,
your ear collects the outgushings
like dewdrop beads on a fairy's necklace.

i, poem, written on vellum
singed by the fire of too close
to the sun, i honour the passage
from cave to incandescent waterfall
crashing at the feet of the master….
quench me.

i, poem, am the coracle
carrying the compassion
of the man, as the winter river
rears up in the clefted valley,
a power more frenzied
than he can express.
his penning
and your reading
release him.

i, poem,
am the thick field
of storm clouds,
and you, receiver,
are the lightening flash,
obscured,
while he, writer,
is the thunder crack
he knows little of
until the alchemy of three
occurs.

in the end you have become

gollum-like
you claw at the bed rails,
tongue slathering,
swiping at intruders
with a wayward hand.

skin grey.
wild eyed.
grimace of a curling lip.

in the end
you have become
a mirror image
of the woman
you so
despised

and your firstborn
the daughter
of two
mon
sters

bacchanalia in the huerta

they got drunk
they got stoned
they ate wild boar
  and the nightingales sang

red wine bloodied the table
protest songs were shouted
dogs fought over flesh
  and almonds grew overhead

the repertoire petered out
conversations became lewd
and sticky

sputum landed
six inches from
my shoe

  i left to view tomatoes
  tall beside their canes

the seasons danced

dance, then, wherever you may be, sang she,
gently swaying, and strumming her
guitar strings in the pink cycladic
skyscape. *i am the lord*
of the dance, said he, sang she,
and her cherub twenty-two year old lips
lapped around each indolent afternoon and all
the day long, age following age.
i danced in the morning
when the world was begun, sang she,
right the way into orange blossom spring
with wild narcissi plucked and folded into
waterfall shimmery hair
streaming over the pinks and yellows
of her sun and moon embroidered blouse
and the unbound breasts beneath. iris
purple saffron on the slopes and cyclamen
to dusky chamomile and fennel, sage,
oregano, and pomegranate flowers
red and sticky. poppies died
and mulberries plopped on rounded stones
where her rickety chair trembled with echoes, *they*
came with me and the dance went on. the
vineyards plumped and juices hung in the air
and there she sat, with oyster thistle, pink oleander
and the corn buntings in the melon shade,
and flagons of red wine were passed
from mouth to mouth, and lizards lazed,
olives ripened, oranges dropped,
and the grapes lay in the sun for seven days.

golden orioles heard her sing, *dance,*
then, and so they paused
on their journey south, *they came with me –*
they supped on figs, bathed

and fluffed and danced for her,
and sky-circled
away to sahel savannahs, crickets
and caterpillars
before the rains came in
and wells filled up
and scorched hillsides fattened,
and still she sang, *when the world was*
begun, sang she, her hair ringletting and dripping,
and droplets of october wet tremoring on lips
a moment while geckos
nibbled at prickly pears
and fires were lit and ancient gods roared
thunder. all through the winter she sang.
she sang with socks on, steaming
mountain tea to hand, *i danced for the fishermen,*
james and john, she sang to the fisherboats
bobbing and anchored
and the ferryboat not docking
in the sea of rise and fall and swish
and spray, and nights followed days and
she watched over islands rufous pink
at dawn and storm cloud silver fade
to grey to mirage merge with water
in the hush of light
to evening, moon to night, and then, and
then, lemon branches budded,
muddied tracks prepared to brittle, grapes
in tiny tautness firmed, and fields
flushed up and wagtails
having crossed the sand dunes
and aegean seascapes, heading
northwards, dipped
for insects. midday rust and heat-hazed
rock turned blue in cooling
sunset, while the long-legged buzzard
hunted for his supper, and scented almond
blossom mixed with garlic and with mandrake.

and if you waited
while the seasons rained
and honeyed, faded, burst,
returned, and if you happened
to be picking thyme nearby, or lowering
a bucket in the well, surveying black
and twist of vines, or contemplating
cassiopeia, you'd hear her, *dance*
then, on and on, *i*
still go on, sings she.

Note: Italics are quoted from *Lord of the Dance* by Sydney Carter

all i need to write

all i need to write is my writing shed
and a window onto nature. then i write the nature
write the window, write the shed. then i write
whatever the space beckons into being.

in my shed i have a sofa, a kettle, slippers and sky.
sky is imperative, as is my laptop, as are oat cakes.
my sellotaped dictionary and covered and re-
covered roget's are permanent residents.

miss atherton taught me the thesaurus. in
a winter classroom with windows onto a
stark and gravelled playground
she encouraged me to look into corners and
at the small things, to hold my gaze, to see further.

perhaps she was a buddhist? a buddhist spinster
english teacher in a very catholic school.

nuns of shrivelled face and age-spot hands gripped
chalk and formulated on blackboards. white chalk to
complement black habits. the chalk of christ no doubt.
scratchily flawless

while my life and i - more black less white, thoroughly
flawed - will always need a space blank but for beauty

to gropingly, nakedly, write out my mind.

b o x e s

the norfolk broads. nice in
winter they say. the spaciousness.
the sky. the wet. i've never been
there - to the sky or the norfolk
broads - but children live, and

some abort, in both. i was once
in norwich. my best friend's father
made boxes. their sprowston red
brick house and the section of
the bird-pecked shed that

wasn't storing seedlings smelled
of cardboard. fathers have their
places. some could be
wrapped tight in gaffer tape,
cartonned up and carted off

for not doing their job well
enough. boxes and houses. all
can flood and get soggy, like
my norfolk girlfriend's mandatory
yellow dress when her period

began in geography class - how
embarrassing was that. the isle
of wight erosion lesson never
did take hold. friends get lost,
end up in zippered pockets of

the mind before a crate in the
ground. dying newborns doing
time in see-through plastic
prisons; IV tubes, a ventilator,
pumping in the possibility of

hope while wrenched open
woman expresses tears and
milk. a coffin with a hole just
wide enough to put a hand
through to touch a baby boy.

old hand

old hand
withering in october light

light like fishes
flashing briefly to the surface

glinting memories
the pieces of her life

un-fit together now
what used to fit so neatly

like the ring
sixty years ago

when she gave herself
to an imagined future

fishes jump through her mind
arching and flopping

the dance they danced
the love they made

the
slaps
black
eyes
his ring
meeting
her cheek
with force

red on white

outside that door
that door of steel
and no window
slumps the foetal woman
long shadowed in the snow
wrists upturned
smooth
veins protruding
it would be a simple
and quick end
red on white
quite
striking

how long does it take
for blood to freeze
at minus three degrees?

pi
sa

it
was
easy
lean
ing in
to you
as if
you
were
the
ether
of ages
and i the
tower of
pisa for
pisa would
i fall on my
face or pisa
would if not
for ether's ag
es holding her
up pisa he pisa
we pisa us leaned
into the wind and
leaned a long way
over and the over
way is over nearly
near we sway to
where i once saw
scarecrow strawy
hair in hay and it
was you my
ancient swirl
of toffee lick
ing loveliness

and never more
will hurricanes
and monsters
ribbons friv
olous in hair
that can't be
serious un
ruly and
as wiggly
unframed
as buses
on the m-
way slith
ering in
oil slick
slither in
my oil
slicks so
stroke me
gentle hold
me strong
like furry
top tufts on
the corn cobs
sit through
freakish aug
ust hailstorm
don't let go and
hearts shall open
more my love my
sweet corn my
ether my love
my
sweet
corn
my
eth
er

anam cara (soul friend)

somewhere we were together, wombing,
two womb souls in closest space.
two heartbeats
incubating
in a golden chamber.

for days and months and maybe years
we floated, punched and grew,
two in one, one cell, touching,
hands that cradled,
feather skim
and whisper
finger fluid
to a palm.

and then the birth.

the folded curtain parted
and we were swept - one left, one right -
into the wings of search and muddy journey
questing what was lost
with just a sense of sketchy knowing
something
wasn't there.
something
wasn't right.

> the irish will tell you that
> to meet anam cara is a blessing;
> the return
> to your place of greatest sacredness
> - home.

finding the mirror soul self,
the echo,
the someone just like you.

seeing the same thing
through the same soul eye,
synergizing
each other's view.

you watched for the one who would talk about life
while lying soft as a july sunset in your arms,
and now, disentangling my vision
from the eyes in the face
resting easily against your chest
i see
from the side
two lovers lying,
she her hand to his belly,
and he his hand to her breast,

and the words
billow on.

> to find anam cara
> is like finding yourself.
> and holding each other
> two hearts are folded,
> fitting like root to earth
> matching like mountain and eagle,
> knowing like you were my words,
> seeing like i were your eyes.

i didn't know just what
or who i looked for
til i knew you
til i saw you
and then i knew
with such a knowing

that the whole green earth
rose as a fist in my soul
with all its seas and deserts, canyons, caves,
and forest canopies
to greet you
walking towards me,
your smile two steps ahead of your body
and your open arms a step in front of that

and here we are.

however perturbed by the world and its worries,
we touch
and instantly we settle,
the old soul remembers
and is no longer split.

> anam cara homecoming reaches
> so deep into the soul
> that some say
> there is nothing more precious in life.

back to where we had been cast from,
and forward after all the scratching on peripheries
of truth,
like we had known each other
since the first winged thing
hatched from the first egg,
as though there had been no evolutionary intervention
of feathered dinosaurs,
dodos, or hummingbirds,

all past lovers have flown,
unmatched, unfitted, undone.

you looked for the moon for your sun,

found.

cuckoos
and hicc
ups

i would have
liked to have inc
ubated your babies,
have you sat upon the n
est of my belly while they
grew their claws and feathers,
their rooting puckers, and their
*are we there yet?*s. i'd have liked
you rubbing my back and trekking
out for kippers at three a.m. - i kno
w you would have done. you would
have put your head to the heartbeat
beneath my boulder belly, come up
dewy eyed, made some joke abou
t cuckoos and hiccups, and writ
ten to the times.

a brief call to say farewell and south you went

passport under junk where the back seat left its shell
bob dylan protesting from detached machine
toothbrush tobacco and a pebble on the dash
cup of earl grey sloshing by the gearstick
basket overflowing with brie avacados dense bread
hoping it won't rain (the window doesn't close)
testing your teeth on dark chocolate digestives…
baling twine and rubber bands holding a life together
while somewhere deep in a crumb specked fraying
pocket of your almost sunbleached jeans the one
way ticket sticks to the fabric and your fingers
as you check for it every few miles, soon kilometres

she waddled

she waddled
into the interminable kitchen
and a bag of walkers
crisps accelerated
her salivary glands. even
the bag crackled and crunched.

oh damn, they come in six packs,
i'll have to eat them all. my
taste buds are really sweating now,
when i should be writing
my memoirs.

that's what they say.
you won't live for ever gran,
and we want to know all your secrets.
.... well i'll be damned if i'll tell them
about the six pack.

so i wait. wait for the blue biro
to write my story for me. what
are you doing
hovering over me, such
a heavy seeming thing?
i am a writer
and as such far superior to you, you
skinny piece of plastic
with delusions of solidity.

the block is heavy. closing
over me, thick
velvet crisp packs over my words.

a life
obliterate.

hideaway

i like this place, my little hideaway where no-one
knows of my existence, or can find me
unless i invite them to. the little den, or tree
or rhododendron bush or paper bag, cardboard
box, sombrero, that the delightful (and
delightfully illustrated) book my grandfather
gave to me - the only book i kept from childhood
incidentally, because i loved the sentiment and
because he gave it to me and he was special and
he took me to brighton and later to paris because *i*
was special too, his first grandchild, yes, to someone
i was special enough to give special things to even if
he couldn't come too close or make
my life a safe one - says every child
should have to hide away in and people
are obliged to tread very quietly around it so
as not to interrupt the one who's hiding   there

treedreaming

at nine, not being allowed to climb trees
or live a life devoid of lady-like apparel
i climbed them in my mind
while strangling pigeon brained mothers
with the shining ironed ribbons she
sadistically
meticulously
tied in bows around my uncatkinned
symmetrical
squeaky clean curls

at seventeen
peers thought i
ought to straighten my hair
wear pan-stick and lip gloss
squeeze
myself into tiny strips of skirts
cleavage heaving cross your hearts and heels so high
on shoes so tight the toes are pinched to screaming

why
i really had no clue

how
would i climb trees in stilettos?

now
i sit in the beech
with my windswept frizz
shrivelling breasts
and clothes as comfortable as the skin i'm in
and my mind flutters
around rainbow flip-flops
forests in slovakia
feet bare on moss sprung grass

the early morning cuckoo
and long-dead mothers

oats

at one end of the seven foot six pitch pine table
handed down from her father (whose children spent days
strapped in prams - god knows how they ever
learned to walk) she ladles organic jumbo oats for market
into crinkly cellophane bags. she weighs them, folds over
the tops satisfyingly, applies sellotape, and labels them,
all the while one eye darting beyond the scales to baby flat
on belly, gurgling gaily, flailing limbs and lifting head
but stationary.

happy baby, happy mother. bags of oats in box -
eighteen, nineteen, and - what? did baby move?
she keeps on weighing, ladling, folding and labelling,
and yes, she's sure that some feet along
the thick, scratched, once blonde wood,
he's pulling up his valiant roundedness
like a very pink and dribbly beached whale

baby, now, can crawl.

clever boy! you crawled! baby can crawl!
(setting him down on the grainy carpet)
one more time? go on, you can do it!

kettle bubbling baby babbling mother
merrily celebrating

and (no prams, no straps) baby moves, again.

by the time the dusky lime blossom warms her lips
baby, stickily coated in puffy, floury flakes, sits
in sack of oats, elated. and, by the time

baby is a teenager, with table due to be passed on
to its next owner, she inscribes on its underside
in purple italics;

In December 1982, on this table, Andrew W first crawled.

my aunt's pigeons

she told me about pigeons.
she had asked her gardener.
why do the pigeons strip the lilac leaves to the veins
at this time of year?
the gardener scratched his head.
no idea. i'll google it, and get back to you.

he didn't.

being a woman who doesn't give up easily she asked him again,
did you google it, then?
he - being of a nervous disposition and believing
her to be as naïve as some other nearly ninety year olds
he had encountered - reddened
and stuttered.

> *certain pigeons*
> *(suffolk)*
> *at certain times of year*
> *(early summer)*
> *at a certain time of day*
> *(evening)*
> *go mad for lilac leaves*
>
> *because*

fidget. twitch. (how can i say this quickly and get it over with?)

> *um,*
>
> *lilac leaf does for pigeons what cannabis does for humans*
> *- it gets them high.*

my aunt, now wryly satisfied, put the matter down.

had she carried it a little further,
delaying her bath, perhaps, she might have enjoyed observing
the effects of the feasts on the cooing columbiformes….

frolicking pigeons, tipsily up-puffing their breasts,
flirtatiously playing, almost giggling,

whilst waddling wiggly paths after ants and worms,
and oo-ing and oogling at the sunset.

my pigeon pursuing aunt.
she might have got hooked.

so he boomeranged

so he boomeranged into my life
brought me that song
was a sunny day
taught it to me
took over the huerto
cooked on the cane-fed fire
tried to sell
the shimmery gems
he had so carefully carried
in cotton handkerchiefs
the eleven thousand miles or so
to the crooks in puerto banus

then flew back
to wollangambe
or bullaburra –
the blue mountains
as if the spanish mountains
weren't quite blue
enough

though as i watched
from the bamboo bowered porch
the layered peace
of the sierra
disappearing into dusk
accompanied by a
time-confused cockerel crowing
in the campo -
the scent
of flores de naranja
and a buzz
of insects filling up
on pomegranate juice
to see them through
till morning

it all seemed
quite
azure and
cornflower cyanic
electric
lazy blue enough
to me

how many mornings does an andalucian insect see?

possibly
more
than the the australian in spain
with his opals and his oatcakes
and his cucumber zucchini red beans green
beans broad beans more beans alcachofa
aubergine growing fingers
sees

pineapple 1

pineapple cool you down
sweet you up, pup.
juice rivers in the sand,
lumpen

pineapple 2

a rivuletting sand dune
wrestles with a pineapple
for supremacy

pineapple wears the crown
tramping up and down the dune
claiming territory

i hereby name this sand dune
pineapple! sod that says the dune –
i name this pineapple sand dune!

wash off the sticky
sticky off the wash
what belongs to what or who

to where to why? and
whose eye and mind decides
a pineapple is not a sand dune?

city streets, pineapple 3

battered deep fried sugared
chinese grease balled pineapples
proliferate in city streets, seeds splatter
in sewers and rats grow golden shells
and smell quite sweet
in city streets

january airfield

you can watch the weather up here
but perhaps there isn't any

steam slick coated picture windows veil
the view like sugar mouse mix thick
and sticky nice for licking if
you were a toddler and your teeth were
not yet rotting

jolly dinky aeroplanes with winter
jackets like the horses and old greyhounds
quieted by mist that takes their wingspan
by a heavy arm and silences
the aviator
engines
whirring props
wind turbines
and ice cream slurpers - back to toddlers
again

so owners stay away or sit
inside all wistful waiting
for a vista to come visible and
mud-locked planes to lift above
the mire of murky january
drinking cappuccino with one eye on
the smoked out fog
obliterated sky
and plains and hills
and planes and plains and
hills and sky
and planes

ashram, wales

the elephant
the lentils
the cabbages
and everything except two bemused women
had been om namah shivaya'd over
and were therefore
sanctified

so in the goddess temple
they got pooja'd –
smeared their heads with
representations of
menstrual fluid and semen
then bathed themselves in fire
before stepping out
– blessed as the dung
and the soft dyfed drizzle

a kiss creeps

emergency. traumatised. jumping. bean. nerves.
body. psychically. battered. emotions. knotty.
frayed. i. cannot. walk. i. cannot. stand. a kiss
creeps under my visor (arm over scarf over post
op eyes). love hops up in a clouded vision. milk.
bleary. glare. hazy. inverted. mirage. iris. too.
open. light. too. bright. will i later see poetry? your
smile? you hold my hand become my
gilead my stillness and my mountain where
i have none. you tingle me to aliveness my january
icicle frost my april bursting blossom. heal
me my bright sighted kiss plopping leaping lamb.

silence is the om

silence is the om that emerges
from the state of no-words

and if one has no words
one is surely not a writer

if i am not a writer
i need no words

i can om all day
for om is not a word

it is, they say
the vibration of the universe

but reader
here is the conundrum

i as your writer
can not attempt to word for you

the om
the vibration of the universe

silence is limitless
and i am not

while amber

while amber gets her lungs up to scratch
her toenails finished off and enough fat laid
to keep her warm on terra firma
(she doesn't know about the underfloor heating yet)
i take the phone to my room prepared for the moment
it will thrash about on the table pulsing its blue siren
and screamingly gatecrash my dreams
to ensure i receive the proclamation
- she's coming!

whereupon i will push my body
from its dark and singular cocoon
attire naked flesh in garments with sleeves
and drive a cold night to read in searing brightness
my new baby sister with her jumping to the ceiling siblings
while she transits from a solitary water world
into one where dimly red and orange peacefulness is lost
the instant she uses those lungs
for the first time

too late now
to turn back
young amber
though you may
spend a lifetime
trying to

to thin

seed it on a thread of threadbare rug that weeps
for feet that trod it - but don't expect a solid outcome.

voices, tones, and pledges, loves caresses, every age
and dawn, new lovers, fresh passion, more promises

to thin. sacrificing warp and weft for worn out feet
and whispers treading, unravelling, trodden, to be trod.

he was the sort of man who

slobbed around spitting while his wobbly
belly overhung his clown sized creased
and crumbed up trousers flecked with
ketchup faintly sausage smelling and
suspended on well stretched elasticated
braces fraying from the daily drudge of
doing for this dour bugger of a café
owner whose moustached flabby face
maintains hour after hour a grimace and
a frown like …. *what madness put me*
here in this godforsaken semi-derelict
tourist resort that never did extend beyond
the stage of dreams of some idealistic
money minded developer and… *why*
did i buy into his greedy vision - a bustling
modern new build seaside mecca - when
all it is is decrepit wretched and i have
sunk like a fool with it and dying on the
sea bed is frankly more inviting damn here
comes a customer…*go away why don't*
you cant you see i have no time or inclination
only temper subdued by my fatness *verpiss*
*dich** person wanting food and drink or i
shall grunt pass wind and overcharge you

* 'piss off' in german

1950's pink

sucking fizzy wafers pink
he loves me
loves
me not
bubble gum and waving
girls by bumper cars
in pulse of fairground
streaking neon rock
around the clock and pink
stilettos
rave and scream and sticky cotton
candy kisses
so much sugar
sugar dandy
sweetheart

baby cham and swirling skirts
with nails all glossy pink
and cheeks
of powder
puffed and mushed
by falls of tears
by fools
in love
and ballads
sung by brylcreemed boys
gyrating
we the jiving
giggling chicks
so fluffy blond and pink
so pink it stinks

mr clarkson

mr clarkson -
you could be me.

i come and sit with you each morning
for fifteen minutes - it is my job.
i hold your hand, clean your specs, check
you've taken your pills, and make
conversation - such as it is.

working with you and others like you, out
of habit as i leave at half past four i tap
my arms and bend and touch my knees
whilst reciting shakespeare to remind myself
that your disease is yours and
i can leave it at the door

i could slip into it so effortlessly you see

like a flounder flopping and belly flipping
in the wooden bowl of a boat
it has been landed in. we
all land somewhere,
sometime, sometimes.
and my boat is a fish boat
and yours can be
the boat fish. fishes
and flights
of fancy into
memories you've lost,
they just unzipped themselves and flitted off -
you'll never catch them now, mr clarkson,
will you? gone, to the land - or the ocean -
of never to be found, until the boat (lifeboat?
now there's a concept) upends
itself, disclosing leaks and

all your secrets spilling out like shoals
of shining thick lipped mullet
without rock to hide
behind or hole to burrow in. a boat of flights
you made or didn't make, things you lost or
never had, but which your brain bit into.

    ....it was a smoggy city in a.... parent, or
    an autumn city in a smog, and parent, you,
    or me, of woolly scarved and mittened children,

    walking them to mother's through
    the orange lamplight
    - didn't we?

    the kids were real enough, janet
    and john....
    or were they the books you
    read to them? hold on, didn't
    you have brothers and sisters by those
    names? or is it my name? am i a john
    or a janet?

    snow and puddles not allowed to jump in,
    neither into piles of autumn leaves, or
    splash, get dirty, wet, stay out too late...
    it's not right, is it. they should be seen
    and not heard. see children, see them.
        i'd like to see them jump in puddles now....
        can you bring them to me? ..... bring my children?

capsized ketches to huddle your
brood, then set them aright, sail
to seas of stories keeling,
railing, reeling
in the lines, the times, the always
was but then it wasn't,

not yet topsy-turveyed wayward tales you
lost or never lived
or even imagined,
mr clarkson.

in assembly

the child in assembly
prises her gritted teeth open one
full centimetre, *our blest redeemer*
comes the small shaky sound, *and his*
that gentle voice we hear.

reverend mother outstretches her hand
and points - *you, you in the middle,*
you are not SINGING.

a quivering reply, *i am, i am singing.*
the wimpled woman rises red faced,
insolent child! LEAVE THE HALL!

so she left her place, and the girls
who she wished would like her
and the teachers who she wished
would see her, and the jesus
who she wished would save her
- the jesus *that calms each fear*

same tears springing, same head
hung low, as when she'd been called
to another room that morning
to be raped

blue and the pluto fly-by

deep blue. cloaks and rules. ruler. beat me not. i
will not be beaten into inky bruises rising to the
surface. heal me. heal my bruises, but not with
tincture of ink – the grey sky would take on a
blue hue to cover the blue bruising of me. um-
brellas windblown inside out not protecting
heads exposed to rain, a storm of ink. clouds
rain blue on sloppy grass, scuzzy. feed a pink
hydrangea blue ink and turn it purple. tish fed
hydrangeas turns smelly. i wouldn't want to
eat or drink blowsy puffy rotting in the rain big
globs of pink. i want to grow in the rain, like
my name, oakwood. this is i. tish hydrangea
does not sound like me, far too fluffy. give
me indigo. lapiz. deep sky. pluto!! ah! pluto!

and now the moon's come up

and now the moon's come up
in the sunny high sky
and my cup of soup
and overheated shed
the lumpily stuffed sofa
and not enough sleep last night
hit me like
a fat and thickly muffled
brick

she eats bananas

she eats bananas while she finishes off the book
the zinc should keep her mentally alert
as her monkey mind darts about
scavenging for peanuts
not nuts but vegetables
and assessing which trivia is too trivial

trivial pursuits never excited her
the way that scrabble and dictionaries did
so life unfurled
bracken from its curl
perhaps not blossoming
but
productive

she travelled and she wrote
kids came and went
she made sure she walked each day
even in fog
of which there was plenty
and she wore three scarves
and here it is
a book
because
the way you approach exercise
is the way you approach life
and a poem
without a reader
is a dead thing

so read
read the loaded eagles
sprung from their shit heaped aviaries
the questions curve-balled back
on the questioner

the sunlight thick with blood
and the moss soft earth
upon which briefly sat
a goddess fat and sumptuous
arranging lovers
gastropods
kippers
and kilometres
into book form
while eating
bananas

www.ingramcontent.com/pod-product-compliance
Lightning Source LLC
Chambersburg PA
CBHW071533080526
44588CB00011B/1660
* 9 7 8 1 9 1 1 4 1 2 8 7 8 *